50 Piano Classics

100 of the World's Most Beloved Masterpieces in Two Volumes

IN THEIR ORIGINAL FORM

SELECTED & EDITED BY E. L. LANCASTER & KENON D. RENFROW

Volume 1: Composers A–G

About This Collection

The 100 pieces (including individual sonatina movements) in these collections have been favorites of pianists and piano students throughout the years. They range from intermediate to advanced levels of difficulty. Complete in two volumes, the first book contains 50 pieces by composers whose last names begin with the letters A through G. The second book contains 50 pieces by composers whose last names begin with the letters H through Z.

Chosen from the four stylistic periods of piano repertoire, all selections are in their original form and have neither been simplified nor arranged. To make the music easier to perform, the editors have realized ornaments and added editorial markings such as phrasing, expression marks, pedal marks, and dynamics where appropriate. The music will provide hours of enjoyment for pianists of all ages. Within each collection, the pieces appear in alphabetical order according to the composer's last name.

Alfred Music Publishing Co., Inc.
P.O. Box 10003
Van Nuys, CA 91410-0003
alfred.com

ISBN-10: 0-7390-7926-3
ISBN-13: 978-0-7390-7926-3

Cover Photos
Piano: © Shutterstock.com / dionis • Rug: © Planet Art

Contents by Composer

Contents by Title (alphabetically)

Tango in D Major
(Espana)

Isaac Albéniz (1860–1909)
Op. 165, No. 2

Gigue
(Partita in B-flat Major)

Johann Sebastian Bach (1685–1750)
BWV 825

ped. simile

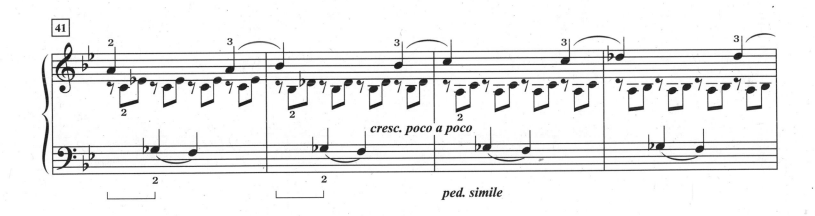

Gavotte

(French Suite No. 5 in G Major)

Johann Sebastian Bach (1685–1750)
BWV 816

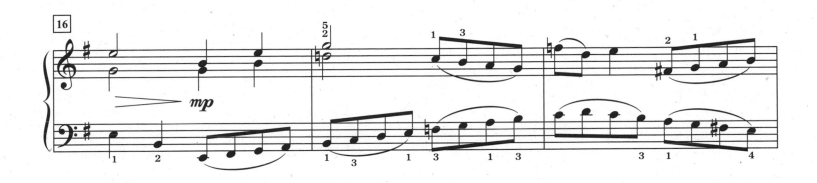

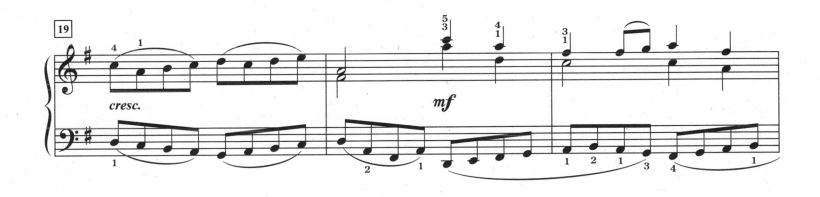

Invention No. 8 in F Major

Johann Sebastian Bach (1685–1750)
BWV 779

Invention No. 13 in A Minor

Johann Sebastian Bach (1685–1750)
BWV 714

Invention No. 14 in B-flat Major

Johann Sebastian Bach (1685–1750)
BWV 785

Prelude and Fugue in C Minor

(The Well-Tempered Clavier, Book 1)

Johann Sebastian Bach (1685–1750)
BWV 847

Fugue

Allegretto moderato

Bear Dance

Béla Bartók
(1881–1945)

Brâul
(Romanian Folk Dances)

Béla Bartók (1881–1945)
Sz. 56, No. 2

Allegro

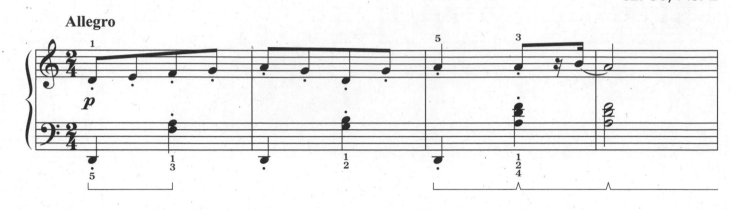

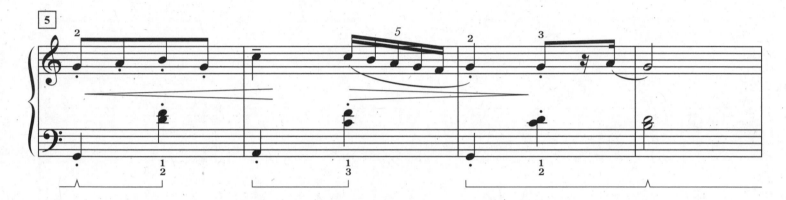

2nd time: poco rit.

Măruntel
(Romanian Folk Dances)

Béla Bartók (1881–1945)
Sz. 56, No. 6

Più allegro

Sonata No. 8 in C Minor

(Pathétique)

(Movement II)

Ludwig van Beethoven (1770–1827)
Op. 13

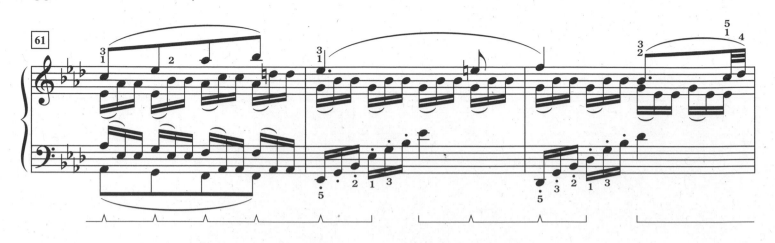

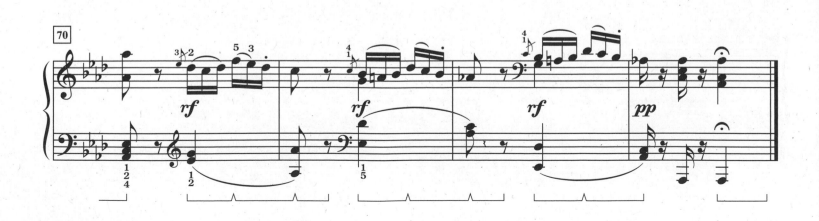

Sonata No. 14 in C-sharp Minor

(Moonlight)

(Movement I)

Ludwig van Beethoven (1770–1827)
Op. 27, No. 2

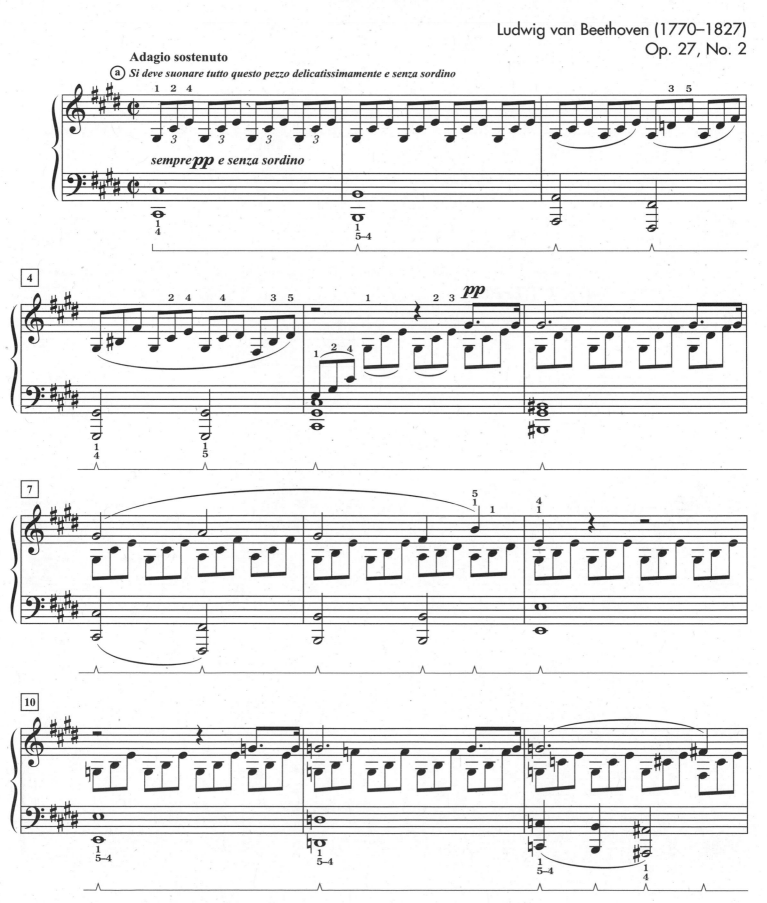

ⓐ This whole piece must be played with the greatest delicacy and with pedal.

Sonatina in F Major
(Movements I & II)

Ludwig van Beethoven
(1770–1827)

Allegro assai

RONDO
Allegro assai

Sonata No. 20 in G Major

(Movements I & II)

Ludwig van Beethoven (1770–1827)
Op. 49, No. 2

Tempo di minuetto

Twelfth Street Rag

Euday Louis Bowman
(1887–1949)

Sonatina in A Minor

Georg Anton Benda
(1722–1795)

Intermezzo in E-flat Major

Johannes Brahms (1833–1897)
Op. 117, No. 1

Intermezzo in A Major

Johannes Brahms (1833–1897)
Op. 118, No. 2

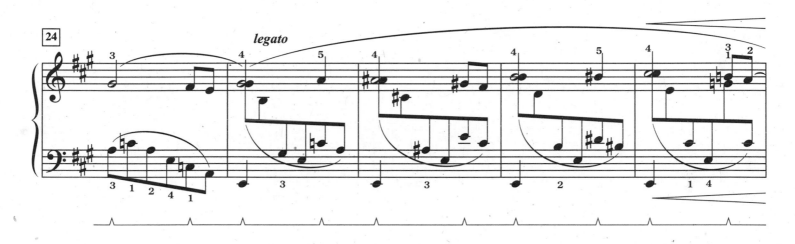

Waltz in A-flat Major

Johannes Brahms (1883–1897)
Op. 39, No. 15

ⓐ Tempo marking is editorial. Brahms gave no tempo indication.

Waltz in E Major

Johannes Brahms (1833–1897)
Op. 39, No. 2

ⓐ Moderately

ⓐ Tempo marking is editorial. Brahms gave no tempo indication.

Nocturne in E Minor

Frédéric Chopin (1810–1849)
Op. 72, No. 1

Nocturne in E-flat Major

Frédéric Chopin (1810–1849)
Op. 9, No. 2

Prelude in E Minor

Frédéric Chopin (1810–1849)
Op. 28, No. 4

Prelude in A Major

Frédéric Chopin (1810–1849)
Op. 28, No. 7

Prelude in C Minor

Frédéric Chopin (1810–1849)
Op. 28, No. 20

Prelude in D-flat Major

(Raindrop)

Frédéric Chopin (1810–1849)
Op. 28, No. 15

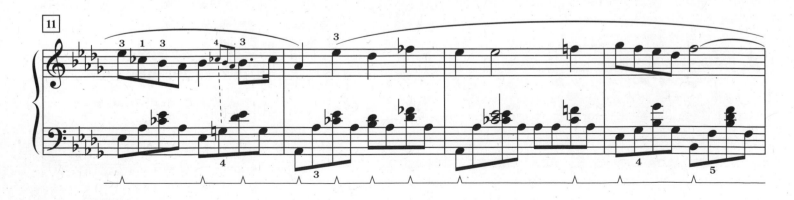

Waltz in A Minor

Frédéric Chopin
(1810–1849)

Waltz in D-flat Major

(Minute)

Frédéric Chopin (1810–1849)
Op. 64, No. 1

Sonatina in C Major
(Movements I & II)

Muzio Clementi (1752–1832)
Op. 36, No. 3

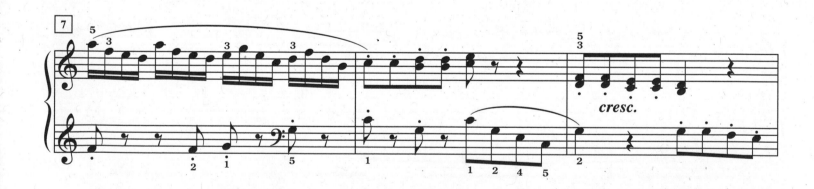

Le Coucou
(The Cuckoo)

Louis-Claude Dacquin
(1694–1772)

First Arabesque

Claude Debussy
(1862–1918)

Tempo rubato (un peu moins vite)

Clair de Lune

(Suite bergamasque)

Claude Debussy
(1862–1918)

Andante
très expressif

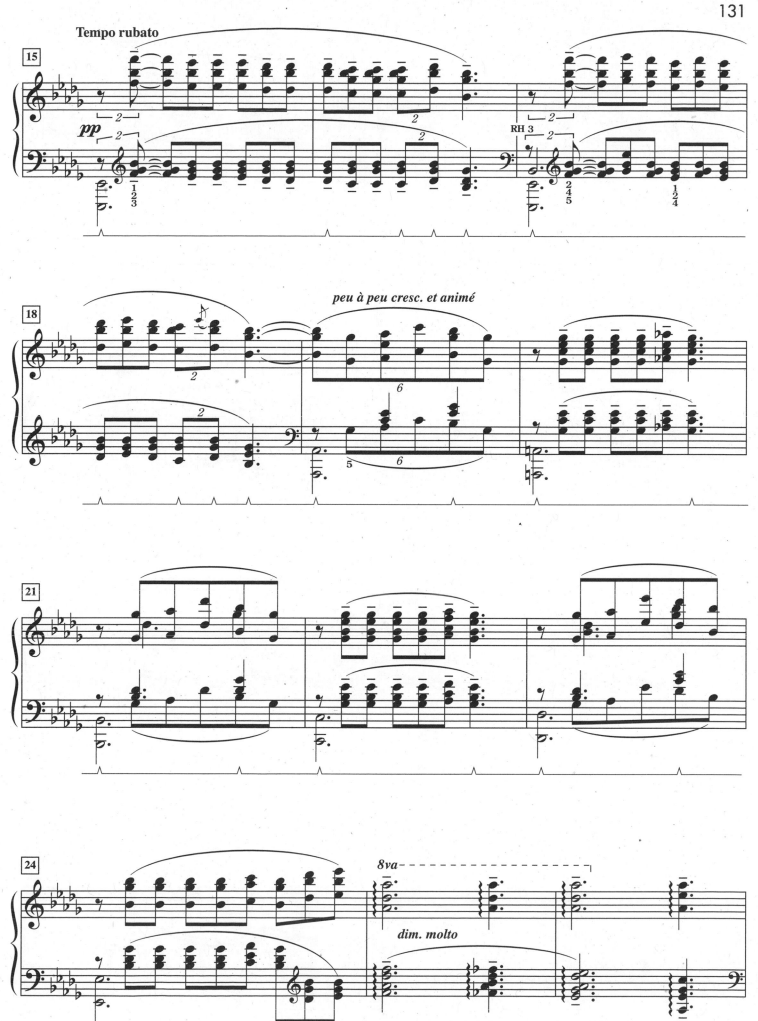

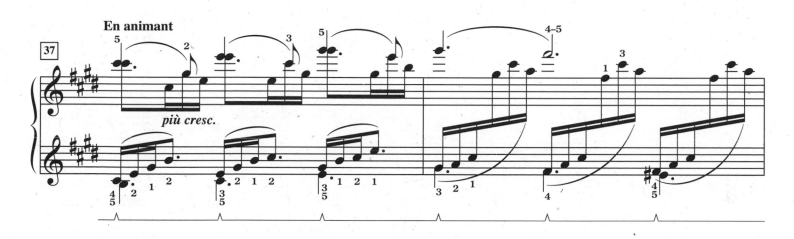

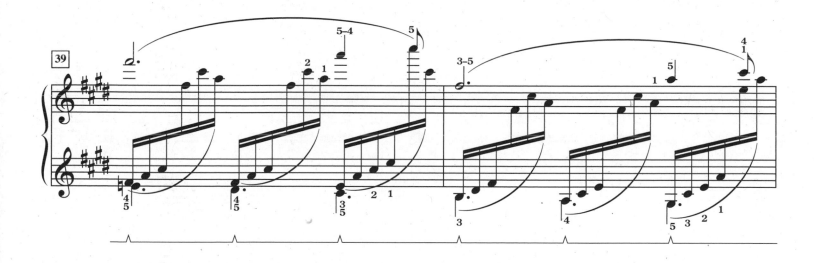

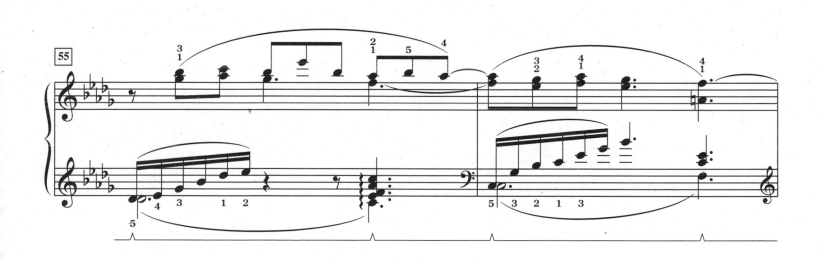

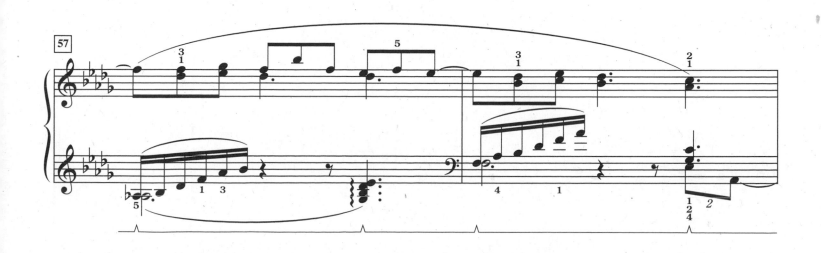

Le fille aux cheveux de lin

(Preludes, Book 1)

Claude Debussy
(1862–1918)

Très calme et doucement expressif

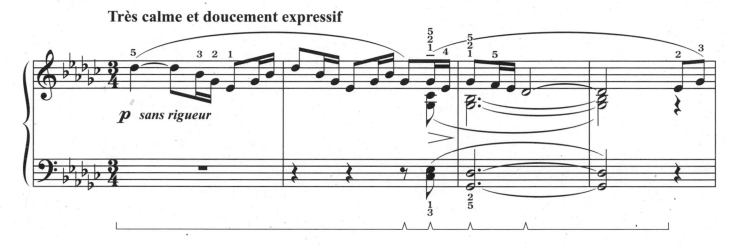

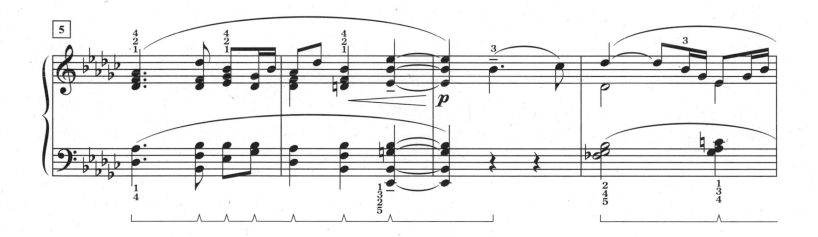

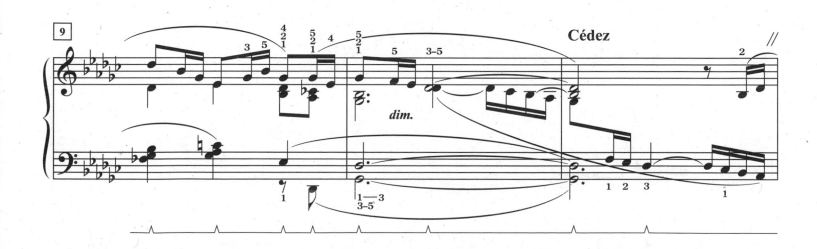

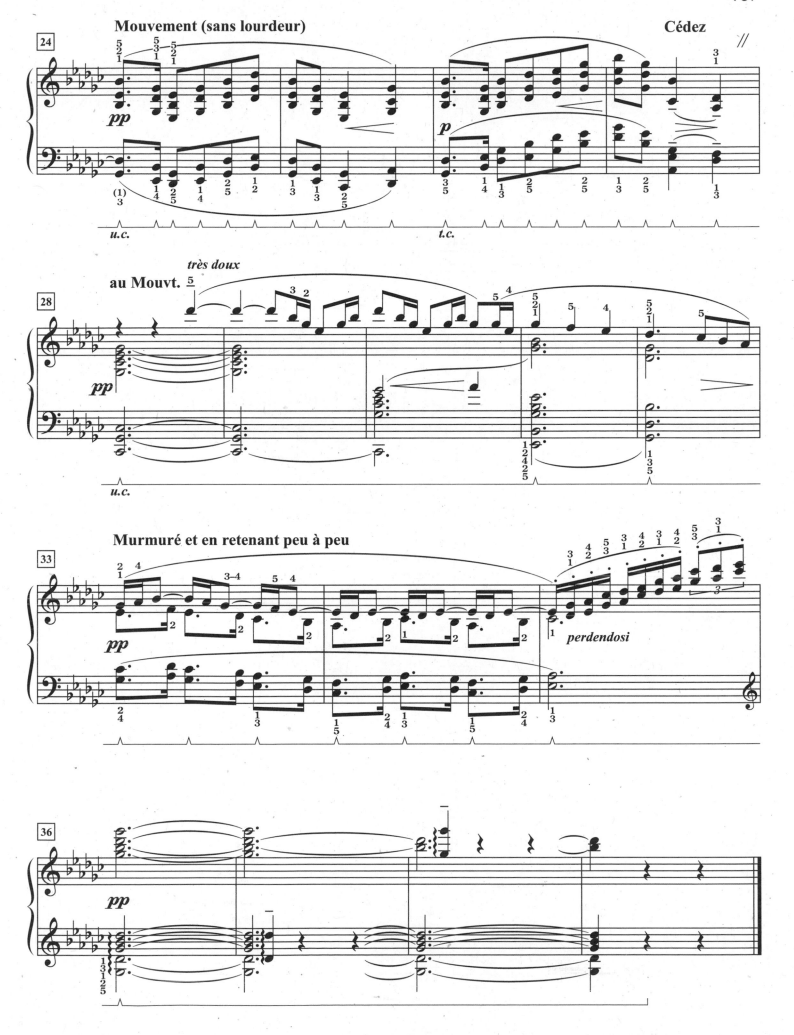

Le petit nègre

Claude Debussy
(1862–1918)

Golliwog's Cakewalk

(Children's Corner)

Claude Debussy
(1862–1918)

Cédez, avec une grande émotion

Rêverie

Claude Debussy
(1862–1918)

Juba
(In the Bottoms)

R. Nathaniel Dett
(1882–1943)

Waltz in E-flat Major

Marie-Auguste Durand (1830–1909)
Op. 83

Salut d'amour

(Liebesgross)

Edward Elgar (1857–1932)
Op. 12

ⓐ Small notes are optional.

Nocturne in B-flat Major

John Field
(1782–1837)

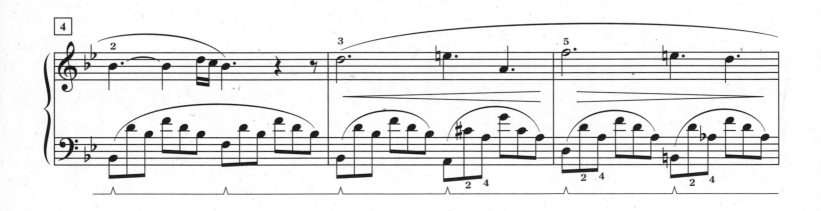

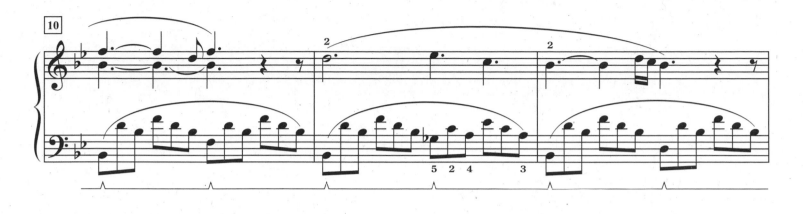

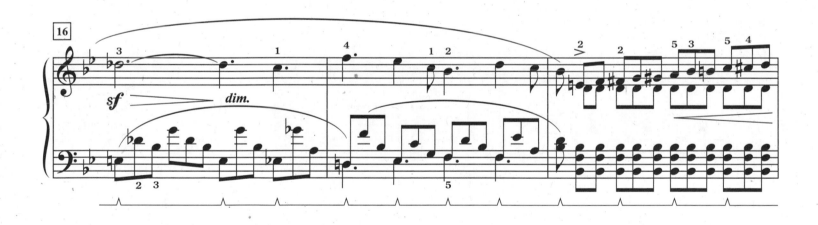

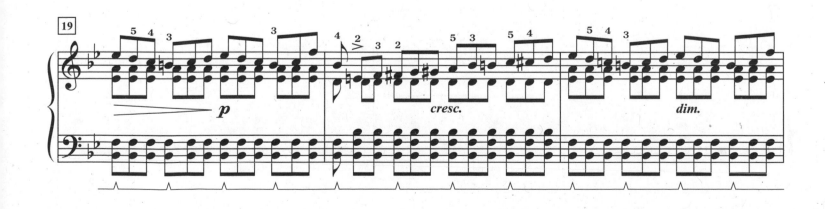

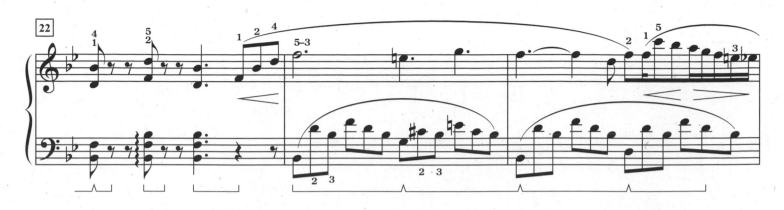

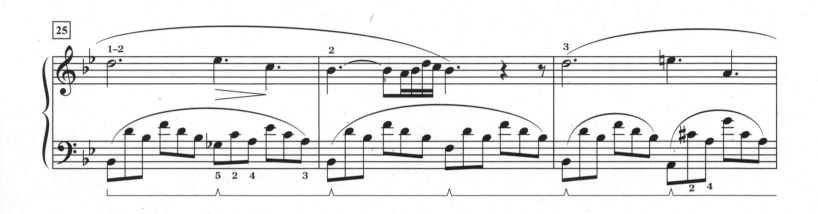

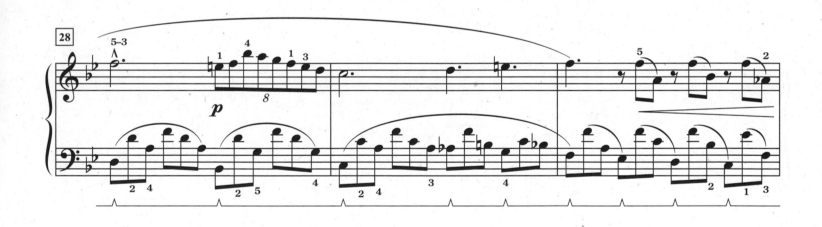

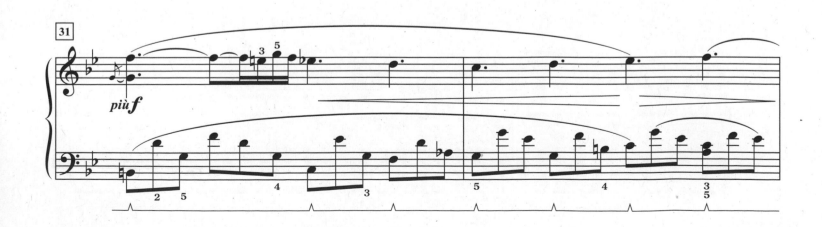

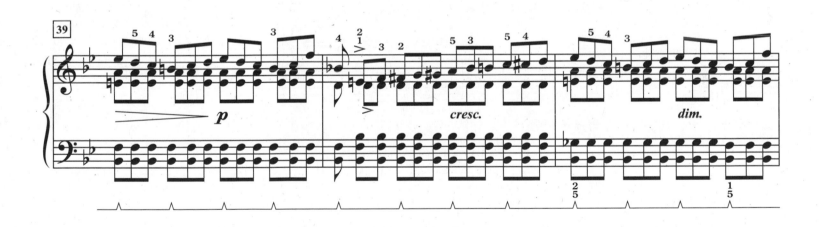

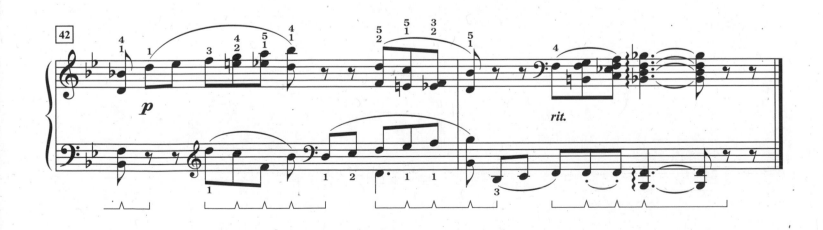

Spanish Dance

Enrique Granados (1867–1916)
Op. 5, No. 5

Andantino, quasi allegretto

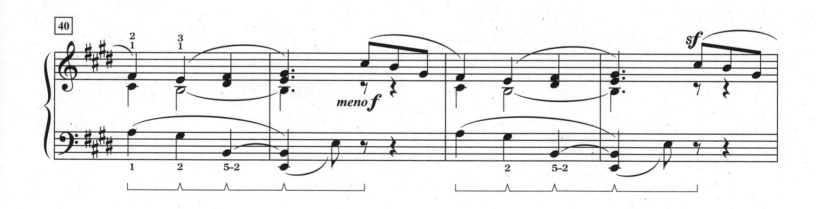

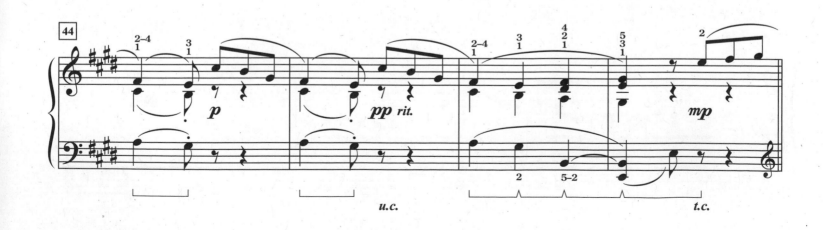

Prelude in D-flat Major

Reinhold Gliere (1875–1956)
Op. 43, No. 1

Elfin Dance

Edvard Grieg (1843–1907)
Op. 12, No. 4

Puck

Edvard Grieg (1843–1907)
Op. 71, No. 3

Notturno

Edvard Grieg (1843–1907)
Op. 54, No. 4

Scherzo in D Minor

Cornelius Gurlitt
(1820–1901)

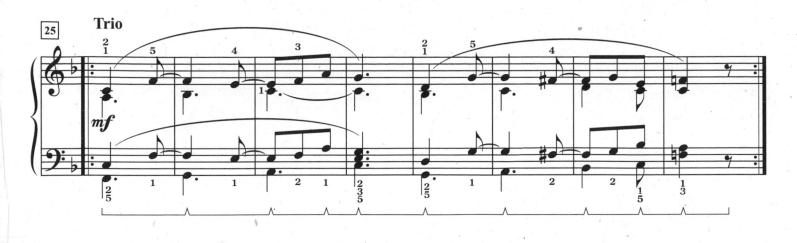

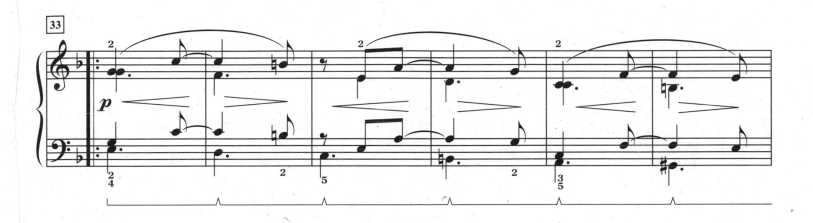

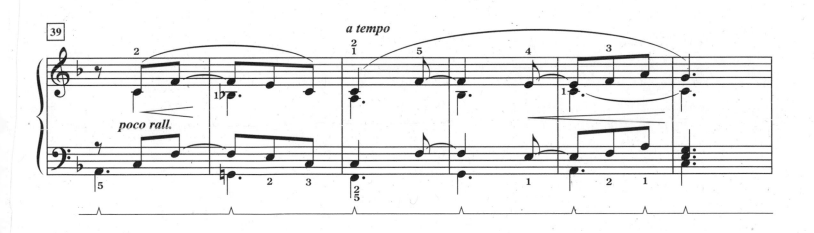

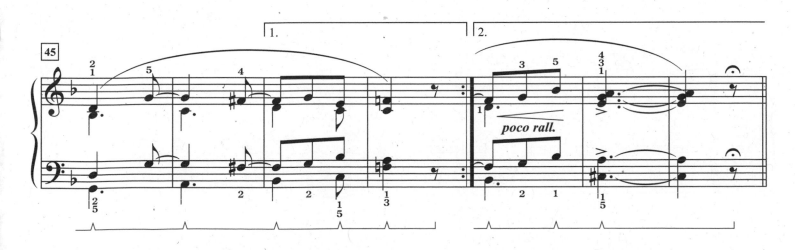

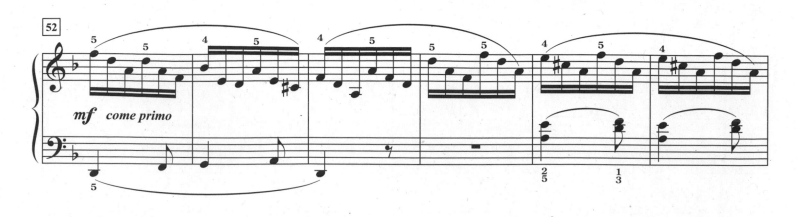

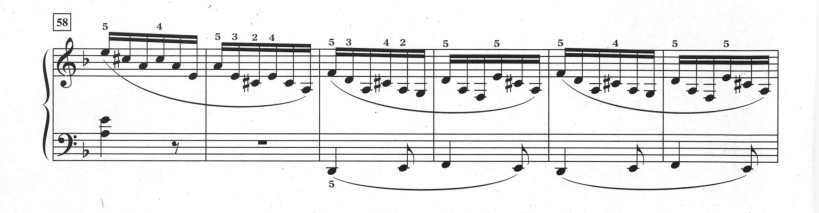

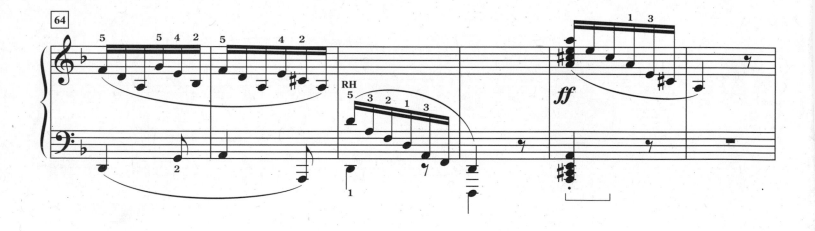

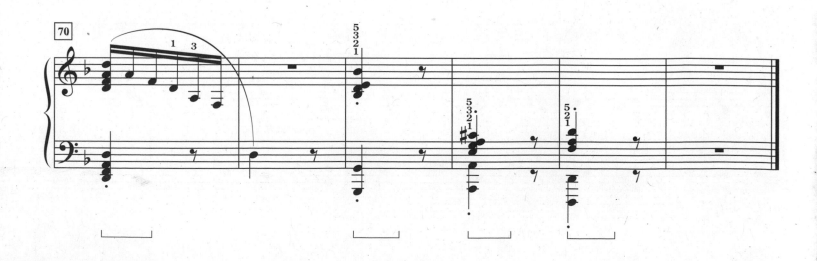